Ingredients for a Balanced Christian Life

Dr. Aaron R. Jones

Ingredients for a Balanced Christian Life

Copyright © 2016

Printed in the United States of America

Published by Kingdom Kaught Publishing, LLC Denton, Maryland

All rights reserved. No part of this book may be reproduced or transmitted in any form or by any means, electronic or mechanical, including photocopying, recording or by any information storage and retrieval system without written permission from the author, except for the inclusion of brief quotations in a review.

All scripture quotations are from the King James Version of the Bible. Thomas Nelson Publishers, Nashville: Thomas Nelson, Inc. 1972.

Editor: Sharon D. Jones

Copy-editing: Kingdom Kaught Publishing

Graphic Designers: Janell McIlwain –JM Virtual Concepts

Cartia Brown-Morgan –Tech-Ayd Solutions

ISBN: 978-0-9961267-4-8

Library of Congress Control Number: 2016961960

TABLE OF CONTENTS

Introduction
1

Balance in Giving
7

Balance in Communication
13

Balance in Emotions
19

Balance in Praise and Worship
25

Balance in Family
31

Balance in Trusting God
37

Balance in Faith
43

Balance in Trials of Life
49

Balance in Evangelism
55

Balance in Outreach
61

Balance in Servanthood
67

Balance in Spiritual Gifts
73

Balance in Peace
79

Balance in Joy
85

Balance in Satan's Attacks
91

Balance in Marriage
97

Balance in Prayer and Fasting
103

Balance in Neighbor
111

Balance in Forgiveness
117

Balance in Grace
123

Balance in Love
129

Conclusion
135

Introduction

In the natural, we try to eat all the right foods and exercise to keep a healthy life. We understand what we put into our body will determine its health status. The body needs certain nutrients to stay healthy, and without these nutrients the body would not operate properly.

In order to live a healthy Christian life, it is not the natural food we need, but spiritual food. This spiritual food is the Word of God. Matthew 4:4 says, "… It is written, man shall not live by bread alone, but by every word that proceedeth out of the mouth of God." God's Word has all the ingredients we need to live balanced lives. Without the Word of God, we could never live the lives God expects. Daily we must put the ingredients needed so we can walk faithfully in God. God's Word is vital to our spiritual and physical health. When we are weak spiritually, one of the main sources of that weakness is a lack of God's Word. Reading and studying God's Word becomes vital to healthy Christian living. The desire of our Heavenly Father is that we eat a balanced spiritual meal daily. We must allow the Holy Spirit to guide us in a healthy spiritual diet.

1Peter 2:2 says, "As newborn babes, desire the sincere milk of the word, that ye may grow thereby." The Apostle Peter declares there should be a desire and maturity of God's Word by every born-again believer, therefore, our healthy Christian living hinges on our desiring and longing for the truths, knowledge, and revelation of God's Word. Just as we desire a good home cooked meal, God wants our desire for His Word to be even greater. Jesus gives us a promise if we "hunger and thirst after His righteousness," we "shall be filled" (Matthew 5:6). God's Word satisfies and strengthens us to live healthy spiritual lives. Above all, God's Word gives us life. Jesus says in John 6:63, "It is the spirit that quickeneth; the flesh profiteth nothing: the words that I speak unto you, they are spirit, and they are life."

We must eat the Word daily and be intentional about our diet. We must understand without a balanced diet, we are in danger of being spiritually malnourished. There are several ways we can eat the Word, starting with these five (5):

(1) Hear the Word

Romans 10:17—"So then faith cometh by hearing, and hearing by the word of God.

(2) Meditate on the Word

Joshua 1:8—"This book of the law shall not depart out of thy mouth; but thou shalt meditate therein day and night, that thou mayest observe to do according to all that is written therein: for then thou shalt make thy way prosperous, and then thou shalt have good success."

(3) Study the Word

2 Timothy 2:15—"Study to shew thyself approved unto God, a workman that needeth not to be ashamed, rightly dividing the word of truth."

(4) Hide the Word

Psalm 119:11—" Thy word have I hid in mine heart, that I might not sin against thee."

(5) Obey the Word

James 1:22—"But be ye doers of the word, and not hearers only, deceiving your own selves."

In the coming chapters, we will look at some ingredients needed to live a balanced Christian life. Each ingredient will have scriptures and self-assessment questions. Upon reading each ingredient, you will decide through the Holy Spirit, if you are truly living a balanced life.

Giving Ingredients

BALANCE IN GIVING

Giving is a key element in our Christian walk. God calls us to give our first-fruits. God not only wants us to give, but give with right attitude (cheerfully). Our tithe is owed to God and our offering is what we feel led through the Holy Spirit to give Him. God reminds us that giving is not an option but a requirement. He lets us know there are blessings attached with our giving. Giving should be an expression of our Christian walk. God holds all resources and He makes us managers over what He allows us to have.

Walking in giving must be a lifestyle.

Ingredients for Giving:

Ingredient #1—Tithes

"Bring ye all the tithes into the storehouse, that there may be meat in mine house, and prove me now herewith, saith the lord of hosts, if I will not open you the windows of heaven, and pour you out a blessing, that there shall not be room enough to receive it."

— Malachi 3:10

Ingredient #2—Firstfruits

"Honour the Lord with thy substance, and with the firstfruits of all thine increase."

— Proverbs 3:9

Ingredient #3—Have a willing heart

"Take ye from among you an offering unto the Lord: whosoever is of a willing heart, let him bring it, an offering of the Lord; gold, and silver, and brass."

— Exodus 35:5

Ingredient #4—Understanding the blessing

"I have shewed you all things, how that so laboring ye ought to support the weak, and to remember the words of the Lord Jesus, how he said, it is more blessed to give than to receive."
— Acts 20:35

Ingredient #5—Be a giver

"Give, and it shall be given unto you; good measure, pressed down, and shaken together, and running over, shall men give into your bosom. For with the same measure that ye mete withal it shall be measured to you again."
— Luke 6:38

Ingredient #6—Give cheerfully

"Every man according as he purposeth in his heart, so let him give; not grudgingly, or of necessity: for God loveth a cheerful giver. And God is able to make all grace abound toward you; that ye, always having all sufficiency in all things, may abound to every good work."
— II Corinthians 9:7, 8

Ingredients for Balanced Christian Living
Recipe for:
GIVING

Malachi 3:10	Tithes
Proverbs 3;9	FIrsttruits
Exodus 35:5	Have a willing heart
Acts 20:35	Understanding the blessing
Luke 6:38	Be a giver
2 Corinthians 9:7, 8	Give cheerfully

Ingredients for Balanced Christian Living

IDENTIFY THE FOLLOWING:

1. What ingredients am I lacking in my giving?

2. What ingredients will I add to my life today?

3. What ingredient do I struggle with the most?

Communication Ingredients

BALANCE IN COMMUNICATION

We are ambassadors of God; and our communication must be one that represents the love and character of God. The Bible indicates there is power in the tongue, and that it is hard to tame. We must remember that we will give an account for every word we speak. What percentage of your conversations is regarding the Gospel? Most people remember your negative words over your positive. God wants us to be His mouthpiece for His Kingdom.

Walking in godly communication must be a lifestyle.

Ingredients for Communication:

Ingredient #1—Accountable to your words

"But I say unto you, that every idle word that men shall speak, they shall give account thereof in the day of judgment."
-Matthew 12:36

Ingredient #2—Speaking the Gospel

"Only let your conversation be as it becometh the gospel of Christ: that whether I come and see you, or else be absent, I may hear of your affairs, that ye stand fast in one spirit, with one mind striving together for the faith of the gospel."
-Philippians 1:27

Ingredient #3—Speaking in grace

"Let your speech be always with grace, seasoned with salt, that ye may know how ye ought to answer every man."
-Colossians 4:6

Ingredient #4—Speaking without covetousness

"Let your conversation be without covetousness; and be content with such things as ye have: for he hath said, I will never leave thee, nor forsake thee."

-Hebrews 13:5

Ingredient #5—Acceptable speech

"Let the words of my mouth and the meditation of my heart, be acceptable in thy sight, O Lord, my strength and my redeemer."

-Psalm 19:14

Ingredients for Balanced Christian Living
Recipe for:

COMMUNICATION

Matthew 12:36	Accountable to your work
Philippians 1:27	Speaking the Gospel
Colossians 4:6	Speaking in grace
Hebrews 13:5	Speaking without covetousness
Psalm 19:14	Acceptable Speech

Ingredients for Balanced Christian Living

IDENTIFY THE FOLLOWING:

1. What ingredients am I lacking in my communication?

2. What ingredients will I add to my life today?

3. What ingredient do I struggle with the most?

Emotional Ingredients

BALANCE IN EMOTIONS

Emotions are given by God, but when they are not under control, the result may be negative. If we allow our emotions to work over time, we will spend less time listening to what God has to say. We know that Jesus operated in emotions, but He did not allow His emotions to affect His assignment. Although Jesus wept for Lazarus, He still raised Lazarus from the dead (John 11:32-44). Emotions can hinder Christians from receiving what God has for us.

Walking in a godly approach to emotions must be a lifestyle.

Ingredients for Emotions:

Ingredient #1—Not fearing man

"In God I will praise his word, in God I have put my trust; I will not fear what flesh can do unto me."

-Psalm 56:4

Ingredient #2—Being anxious for nothing

"Be anxious for nothing; but in every thing by prayer and supplication with thanksgiving let your requests be made known unto God."

-Philippians 4:6

Ingredient #3—Not going to bed angry

"Be ye angry, and sin not: let not the sun go down upon your wrath."

-Ephesians 4:26

Ingredients #4—Mind to overcome negativity

"Finally, brethren, whatsoever things are true, whatsoever things are honest, whatsoever things are just, whatsoever things

are pure, whatsoever things are lovely, whatsoever things are of good report; if there be any virtue, and if there be any praise, think on these things."

-Philippians 4:8

Ingredient #5—Joy in trials

"My brethren, count it all joy when ye fall into divers temptations."

-James 1:2

Ingredients for Balanced Christian Living
Recipe for:

EMOTIONS

Psalm 56:4	Not fearing man
Philippians 4:6	Being anxious for nothing
Ephesians 4:26	Not going to be angry
Philippians 4:8	Mind to overcome negativity
James 1:2	Joy in trials

Ingredients for Balanced Christian Living

IDENTIFY THE FOLLOWING:

1. What ingredients am I lacking in my emotions?

2. What ingredients will I add to my life today?

3. What ingredient do I struggle with the most?

Balance in Praise and Worship

God is a holy God. As Christians we must acknowledge Him in all that we do. God is the only one worthy of our praise, worship and adoration. Our praise and worship takes the focus off ourselves and places it on God. Our acknowledgment of God should not be based on feeling, but based on a need to give back what He has given us. Praise and worship is more than singing; it is a lifestyle. It is not just a moment, but all eternity.

Walking in praise and worship must be a lifestyle.

Ingredients for Praise and Worship:

Ingredient #1—Always thanking God

"Giving thanks always for all things unto God and the Father in the name of our Lord Jesus Christ."
                                             -Ephesians 5:20

Ingredient #2—Rejoicing in the Lord

"Rejoice in the Lord always: and again I say, Rejoice."
                                             -Philippians 4:4

Ingredient #3—Give glory to God

"Give unto the Lord the glory due unto his name; worship the Lord in the beauty of holiness."
                                             -Psalm 29:2

Ingredient #4—Worship in Spirit and Truth

"God is a Spirit: and they that worship him must worship him in spirit and in truth."
                                             -John 4:24

Ingredient #5—Blessing the Lord

"I will bless the Lord at all times: his praise shall continually be in my mouth."

-Psalm 34:1

 **Ingredients for Balanced Christian Living**
Recipe for:

PRAISE AND WORSHIP

Ephesians 5:20	Always thanking God
Philippians 4:4	Rejoicing in the Lord
Psalm 29:2	Giving glory to God
John 4:24	Worship in Spirit and Truth
Psalm 34:1	Blessing the Lord

Ingredients for Balanced Christian Living

IDENTIFY THE FOLLOWING:

1. What ingredients am I lacking in my praise and worship?

2. What ingredients will I add to my life today?

3. What ingredient do I struggle with the most?

Family Ingredients

BALANCE IN FAMILY

Ingredients for Dealing with Family Members

Christians are to honor, respect, and love family members. When God instituted marriage, He instituted family. God takes family very serious. Your family should always be one of your first priorities. The Bible has identified the importance of taking care of family and ministry. Family relations are the tools God uses to teach love, obedience, and self-discipline.

Walking in a godly approach to family must be a lifestyle.

Ingredients for family:

Ingredient #1--Obeying Parents

"Children, obey your parents in the Lord: for this is right. Honor thy father and mother; (which is the first commandment with promise). That it may be well with thee and thou mayest live long on the earth."

-Ephesians 6:1-3

Ingredient #2—Multiply and Subdue the earth

"And God blessed them, and God said unto them, Be fruitful, and multiply, and replenish the earth, and subdue it."

-Genesis 1:28

Ingredients #3—Training children

"Train up a child in the way he should go: and when he is old, he will not depart from it."

-Proverbs 22:6

Ingredients #4—Teach the love of God always

"Hear O Israel: The Lord our God is one Lord. And thou shalt love the Lord thy God with all thine heart, and with all thy soul, and with all thy might. And these words which I command thee this day, shall be in thine heart. And thou shalt teach them diligently unto thy children, and shalt talk of them when thou sittest in thine house, and when thou walkest by the way, and when thou lies down, and when thou risest up."

-Deuteronomy 6:4-7

Ingredients #5—Provoke not your children

"And, ye fathers, provoke not your children to wrath: but bring them up in the nurture and admonition of the Lord."

-Ephesians 6:4

**Ingredients for Balanced Christian Living
Recipe for:**

FAMILY

Ephesians 6:1-3	Obeying Parents
Genesis 1:28	Multiply and Subdue the earth
Proverbs 22:6	Training Children
Deuteronomy 6:4-7	Teach the love of God always
Ephesians 6:4	Provoke not your children

Ingredients for Balanced Christian Living

IDENTIFY THE FOLLOWING:

1. What ingredients am I lacking in my family?

2. What ingredients will I add to my life today?

3. What ingredient do I struggle with the most?

Trusting God Ingredients

Balance in Trusting God

Trusting in God to fulfill His Word, plan, purpose, and promises are paramount for the believer. In the natural, trust is hard to obtain but very easy to lose. God's desire is for every believer to trust Him with all their hearts and leave no room for doubt. When trouble or hard times come in our lives, trusting God is vital. Steadfast trust in God will keep the heart from trouble.

Walking in trust for God must be a lifestyle.

Ingredients for Trusting God:

Ingredient #1—Trust God with your whole heart

"Trust in the Lord with all thine heart; and lean not unto thine own understanding."

-Proverbs 3:5

Ingredient #2—Trust God's Word

"And now, O Lord GOD, thou art that God, and thy words be true, and thou hast promised this goodness unto thy servant:"

-2 Samuel 7:28

Ingredient #3—Trust in God's Mercy and Salvation

"But I have trusted in thy mercy; my heart shall rejoice in thy salvation."

-Psalm 13:5

Ingredient #4—Trust in the Name of the Lord

"Some trust in chariots and some in horses, but we trust in the name of the LORD our God."

-Psalm 20:7

Ingredient #5—Trust to keep your heart from trouble

"Let not your heart be troubled: ye believe in God, believe also in me."

-John 14:1

**Ingredients for Balanced Christian Living
Recipe for:**

TRUSTING GOD

Proverbs 3:5	Trusting God with your whole heart
II Samuel 7:28	Trust God's Words
Psalm 13:5	Trust God's Mercy and Salvation
Psalm 20:7	Trust in the Name of the Lord
John 14:1	Trust to keep your heart from trouble

Ingredients for Balanced Christian Living

IDENTIFY THE FOLLOWING:

1. What ingredients am I lacking in my trusting God?

2. What ingredients will I add to my life today?

3. What ingredient do I struggle with the most?

Faith Ingredients

BALANCE IN FAITH

Our faith in God is what leads and guides our lives as believers. Our faith should cause us to believe when we don't see, feel, or hear God. Faith must be an intentional lifestyle: talk faith, walk faith, and live in faith. Our eternal life is based on our belief in the work of Jesus Christ on the cross.

Walking in faith must be a lifestyle.

Ingredients for Faith:

Ingredient # 1—Believing God when we cannot see God

"Now faith is the substance of things hoped for, the evidence of things not seen."

-Hebrews 11:1

Ingredient #2—Walking by faith

"(For we walk by faith, not by sight:)"

-2 Corinthians 5:7

Ingredients #3—Saving Faith

"For by grace are ye saved through faith; and that not of yourselves: it is the gift of God."

-Ephesians 2:8

Ingredient #4—Asking in faith

"But let him ask in faith, nothing wavering. For he that wavereth is like a wave of the sea driven with the wind and tossed."

-James 1:6

Ingredient #5—Pleasing God with our faith

"But without faith it is impossible to please him: for he that cometh to God must believe that he is, and that he is a rewarder of them that diligently seek him."
-Hebrews 11:6

Ingredients for Balanced Christian Living
Recipe for:

FAITH

Hebrews 11:1	Believing God when we cannot see God
2 Corinthians 5:7	Walking by faith
Ephesians 2:8	Saving Faith
James 1:6	Asking in faith
Hebrews 11:6	Pleasing God with our faith

Ingredients for Balanced Christian Living

IDENTIFY THE FOLLOWING:

1. What ingredients am I lacking in my faith?

2. What ingredients will I add to my life today?

3. What ingredient do I struggle with the most?

Trials of Life Ingredients

BALANCE IN TRIALS OF LIFE

Trials are a part of life. God never promised that life with Him would be void of trials, but He did promise to be with us. God has a plan for every trial of the believer. Our trials do not catch God off guard. We must learn to be patient in our trials of life. God will walk with us through every trial.

Walking with a godly approach to the trials of life must be a lifestyle.

Ingredients for Trials of Life:

Ingredient #1—Patient in trials

"Rejoicing in hope; patient in tribulation; continuing instant in prayer."

-Romans 12:12

Ingredient #2—Weapons have no authority

"No weapon that is formed against thee shall prosper; and every tongue that shall rise against thee in judgment thou shalt condemn. This is the heritage of the servants of the LORD, and their righteousness is of me, saith the LORD."

-Isaiah 54:17

Ingredient #3—Deliverence for all trials

"Many are the afflictions of the righteous: but the LORD delivereth him out of them all."

-Psalm 34:19

Ingredient # 4—God will lift up a standard

"So shall they fear the name of the LORD from the west, and his glory from the rising of the sun. When the enemy shall come in like a flood, the Spirit of the LORD shall lift up a standard against him."

-Isaiah 59:19

Ingredient #5—Trials work together

"And we know that all things work together for good to them that love God, to them who are the called according to his purpose."

-Romans 8:28

Ingredients for Balanced Christian Living
Recipe for:

TRIALS OF LIFE

Romans 12:12	Patient in trials
Isaiah 54:17	Weapons have no authority
Psalm 34:19	Deliverance for all trials
Isaiah 59:19	God will lift up a standard
Romans 8:28	Trials work together

Ingredients for Balanced Christian Living

IDENTIFY THE FOLLOWING:

1. What ingredients am I lacking in my trials?

2. What ingredients will I add to my life today?

3. What ingredient do I struggle with the most?

Evangelism Ingredients

Balance in Evangelism

We are not all called to be an Evangelist, but we are all called to evangelize the world. Jesus makes it very clear, that we are to go out and spread the good news of His sacrifice on the cross. We are not to be the decider of whom we will approach. Let the Holy Spirit lead you and obey His leading. The Great Commission is the mission of the Church, there shouldn't be another mission that supersedes it. We are called to be the light of the world. We are not ashamed of the gospel of Jesus Christ (Romans 1:16).

Walking in evangelism must be a lifestyle.

Ingredients for Evangelism:

Ingredient #1—Fulfilling the Great Commission

"Go ye therefore, and teach all nations, baptizing them in the name of the Father, and of the Son, and of the Holy Ghost. Teaching them to observe all things whatsoever I have commanded you: and lo, I am with you always even unto the end of the world. Amen."

-Matthew 28:19, 20

Ingredient #2—Witnessing to anyone

"And he said unto them, Go ye unto all the world, and preach the gospel to every creature."

-Mark 16:15

Ingredient #3—Fulfilling the Great Command

"But ye shall receive power, after the Holy Ghost is come upon you: and ye shall be witnesses unto me both in Jerusalem, and in all Judaea and in Samaria, and unto the uttermost part of the earth."

-Acts 1:8

Ingredient #4—Allowing God to give the increase

"I have planted, Apollos watered; but God gave the increase."
-I Corinthians 3:6

Ingredients #5—Being a laborer of the harvest

"Then saith he unto his disciples, The harvest truly is plenteous, but the labourers are few;"
-Matthew 9:37

Ingredients for Balanced Christian Living
Recipe for:

EVANGELISM

Matthew 28:19, 20	Fulfilling the Great Commission
Mark 16:15	Witnessing to anyone
Acts 1:8	Fulfilling the Great Command
1 Corinthians 3:6	Allowing God to give the increase
Matthew 9:37	Being a laborer of the harvest

Ingredients for Balanced Christian Living

IDENTIFY THE FOLLOWING:

1. What ingredients am I lacking in my evangelism?

2. What ingredients will I add to my life today?

3. What ingredient do I struggle with the most?

Outreach Ingredients

Balance in Outreach

The Church in many ways is the outreached Hand of God. The Church must go outside its walls, if it wants to be successful in outreach ministry. The very foundation of outreach comes from the love of God. God's approach to outreach is "all."

Walking in outreach must be a lifestyle.

Ingredients for Outreach:

Ingredient #1—Understanding God's plan for outreach

"For God so loved the world, that he gave his only begotten Son, that whosoever believeth in him should not perish, but have everlasting life."

-John 3:16

Ingredient #2—Fulfilling the call to outreach

"For I was an hungred, and ye gave me meat: I was thirsty, and ye gave me drink: I was a stranger, and ye took me in: Naked, and ye clothed me: I was sick, and ye visited me: I was in prison, and ye came unto me.

-Matthew 25:35, 36

Ingredient #3—Practice longsuffering to all

"The Lord is not slack concerning his promise, as some men count slackness; but is longsuffering to us-ward, not willing that any should perish, but that all should come to repentance."

-II Peter 3:9

Ingredient #4—Sharing the knowledge of truth

"Who will have all men to be saved, and to come unto the knowledge of the truth."
-I Timothy 2:4

Ingredient #5—Remain salty

"Ye are the salt of the earth: but if the salt have lost his savour, wherewith shall it be salted? it is thenceforth good for nothing, but to be cast out, and to be trodden under foot of men."
-Matthew 5:13

Ingredients for Balanced Christian Living
Recipe for:

OUTREACH

John 3:16	Understanding God's plan for outreach
Matthew 25:35, 36	Fulfilling the call to outreach
II Peter 3:9	Practice longsuffering to all
I Timothy 2:4	Sharing the knowledge of truth
Matthew 5:13	Remain salty

Ingredients for Balanced Christian Living

IDENTIFY THE FOLLOWING:

1. What ingredients am I lacking in my outreach?

2. What ingredients will I add to my life today?

3. What ingredient do I struggle with the most?

Servanthood Ingredients

Balance in Servanthood

The greatest call of a believer is to be called a servant. The life and role of each believer is to be a servant of God. We are obligated to submit to the authority of our Lord and Savior, Jesus Christ. No matter what title a believer holds, it never eliminates the assignment of a servant.

Walking in servanthood must be a lifestyle.

Ingredients of Servanthood:

Ingredient #1—Serving your neighbor

"Let no man seek his own, but every man another's wealth."
-1 Corinthians 10:24

Ingredient #2—Showing greatness in serving

"But he that is greatest among you shall be your servant."
Matthew 23:11

Ingredient #3—Praising the Lord

"Praise ye the LORD. Praise, O ye servants of the LORD, praise the name of the LORD."
-Psalm 113:1

Ingredient #4—Enduring hard times

"But in all things approving ourselves as the ministers of God, in much patience, in afflictions, in necessities, in distresses,"
-2 Corinthians 6:4

Ingredient #5—Coming to serve

"For even the Son of man came not to be ministered unto, but to minister, and to give his life a ransom for many."
-Mark 10:45

Ingredients for Balanced Christian Living
Recipe for:

SERVANTHOOD

1 Corinthians 10:24	Serving your neighbor
Matthew 23:11	Showing greatness in serving
Psalm 113:1	Praising the Lord
2 Corinthians 6:4	Enduring hard times
Mark 10:45	Coming to serve

Ingredients for Balanced Christian Living

IDENTIFY THE FOLLOWING:

1. What ingredients am I lacking in my servanthood?

2. What ingredients will I add to my life today?

3. What ingredient do I struggle with the most?

Spiritual Gifts Ingredients

BALANCE IN SPIRITUAL GIFTS

God has deposited in every believer a gift to be used for the building of His Kingdom. Our gifts should not be self-serving. Our gifts are not used to put on platforms or pedestals to impress mankind. God is strategic through the Holy Spirit to anoint us with such gifts. We are to use our gifts to equip, to encourage, and to edify the body of Christ. God has a plan for using His gifts in us. We have to wait on Him.

Walking in our spiritual gifts must be a lifestyle.

Ingredients for Spiritual Gifts:

Ingredients #1—Making room for your gift

"A man's gift maketh room for him, and bringeth him before great men."

-Proverbs 18:16

Ingredient #2—Manifesting the gifts

"But the manifestation of the Spirit is given to every man to profit withal."

-1 Corinthians 12:7

Ingredient #3—Birthing of gifts

"But all these worketh that one and the selfsame Spirit, dividing to every man severally as he will."

-1 Corinthians 12:11

Ingredient #4—Having gifts

"Having then gifts differing according to the grace that is given to us, whether prophecy, let us prophesy according to the proportion of faith."

-Romans 12:6

Ingredient #5—Serving with your gifts

"As every man hath received the gift, even so minister the same one to another, as good stewards of the manifold grace of God."

-I Peter 4:10

Ingredient #6—Stirring up the gift

"Wherefore I put thee in remembrance that thou stir up the gift of God, which is in thee by the putting on of my hands."

-II Timothy 1:6

Ingredients for Balanced Christian Living Recipe for:

SPIRITUAL GIFTS

Proverbs 18:16	Making room for your gift
1 Corinthians 12:7	Manifesting the gift
1 Corinthians 12:11	Birthing of gifts
Romans 12:6	Having gifts
1 Peter 4:10	Serving with your gift
2 Timothy 1:6	Stirring up your gift

Ingredients for Balanced Christian Living

IDENTIFY THE FOLLOWING:

1. What ingredients am I lacking in my spiritual gifts?

2. What ingredients will I add to my life today?

3. What ingredient do I struggle with the most?

Peace Ingredients

BALANCE IN PEACE

The peace of God is the key to a sound mind. Without godly peace, this Christian life becomes a challenge. We must learn that the peace this world provides is a temporary peace. It will not last through the trends of life. God wants His peace to saturate our mind, body, and soul.

Walking in peace must be a lifestyle.

Ingredients for Peace:

Ingredient #1—Unwavering Peace

"Peace I leave with you, my peace I give unto you: not as the world giveth, give I unto you. Let not your heart be troubled, neither let it be afraid."

-John 14:27

Ingredient #2—Following Peace

"Let us therefore follow after the things which make for peace, and things wherewith one may edify another."

-Romans 14:19

Ingredient #3—Sustaining Peace

"And the peace of God, which passeth all understanding, shall keep your hearts and minds through Christ Jesus."

-Philippians 4:7

Ingredient #4—Ruling Peace

"And let the peace of God rule in your hearts, to the which also ye are called in one body; and be ye thankful."
                                        -Colossians 3:15

Ingredient #5—Loving Peace

"Great peace have they which love thy law: and nothing shall offend them."
                                        -Psalm 119:165

Ingredient #6—Staying Peace

"Thou wilt keep him in perfect peace, whose mind is stayed on thee: because he trusteth in thee."
                                        -Isaiah 26:3

Ingredients for Balanced Christian Living
Recipe for:

PEACE

John 14:27	Unwavering Peace
Romans 14:19	Follow Peace
Philippians 4:7	Sustaining Peace
Colossians 3:15	Ruling Peace
Psalm 119:165	Loving Peace
Isaiah 26:3	Staying Peace

Ingredients for Balanced Christian Living

IDENTIFY THE FOLLOWING:

1. What ingredients am I lacking in my peace?

2. What ingredients will I add to my life today?

3. What ingredient do I struggle with the most?

Joy Ingredients

BALANCE IN JOY

Oftentimes we confuse joy with happiness. Happiness is normally based upon happenings, but joy is based on a relationship with Jesus. As Christians, Jesus wants us to walk in the fullness of His joy. Joy will take us through the hardest trials of our lives. Joy keeps us focused on God and not people or things. Walking in joy must be a lifestyle.

Walking in joy must be a lifestyle.

Ingredients for Joy:

Ingredient #1—Strengthening Joy

"Then he said unto them, go your way, eat the fat, and drink the sweet, and send portion unto them for whom nothing is prepared: for this day is holy unto our Lord: neither be ye sorry; for the joy of the Lord is your strength."

-Nehemiah 8:10

Ingredient #2—Counting Joy

"My brethren, count it all joy when ye fall into divers temptations."

-James 1:2

Ingredient #3—Filling Joy

"Now the God of hope fill you with all joy and peace in believing, that ye may abound in hope, through the power of the Holy Ghost."

-Romans 15:13

Ingredient #4—Sacrificing Joy

> *"And now shall mine head be lifted up above mine enemies round about me: therefore will I offer in his tabernacle sacrifices of joy; I will sing, yea, I will sing praises unto the LORD."*
>
> -Psalm 27:6

Ingredient #5—Worshipping Joy

> *"O clap your hands, all ye people; shout unto God with the voice of triumph."*
>
> -Psalm 47:1

Ingredients for Balanced Christian Living
Recipe for:
JOY

Nehemiah 8:10	Strengthening Joy
James 1:2	Counting Joy
Romans 15:13	Filling Joy
Psalm 27:6	Sacrificing Joy
Psalm 47:1	Worshipping Joy

Ingredients for Balanced Christian Living

IDENTIFY THE FOLLOWING:

1. What ingredients am I lacking in my joy?

2. What ingredients will I add to my life today?

3. What ingredient do I struggle with the most?

Satan's Attack Ingredients

Balance in Satan's Attacks

The Bible tells us in Isaiah 14:12-14 that Lucifer (Satan) was attempting to exalt himself above God. This is the reason why God removed Satan from His Presence. When Satan left the Presence of God he came to earth. Satan became the catalyst for all sin through Adam and Eve. When we deal with the enemy, it is warfare and it should not be taken lightly. God has given us the authority over Satan through Jesus Christ. God has equipped us to fight Satan with the Word of God and the Name of Jesus. We must not allow Satan to bring our lives out of balance with God.

Walking in against Satan's attacks must be a lifestyle.

Ingredients for Satan's Attacks:

Ingredient #1—Putting on God's Armor

"Stand therefore, having your loins girt about with truth, and having on the breastplate of righteousness. And your feet shod with the preparation of the gospel of peace. Above all, taking the shield of faith, wherewith ye shall be able to quench, all the fiery darts of the wicked. And take the helmet of salvation, and the sword of the Spirit, which is the word of God. Praying always with all prayer and supplication in the Spirit…"

-Ephesians 6:14-18

Ingredient #2—Having the right pursuit

"Depart from evil, and do good; seek peace, and pursue it."

-Psalm 34:14

Ingredient #3—Escaping Temptation

"There hath no temptation taken you but such as is common to man: but God is faithful, who will not suffer you to be tempted above that ye are able; but will with the temptation also make a way to escape, that ye may be able to bear it."

-I Corinthians 10:13

Ingredient #4—Abstaining from evil

"Abstain from all appearance of evil."
-I Thessalonians 5:22

Ingredient #5—Running from lust

"Flee also youthful lusts: but follow righteousness, faith, charity, peace, with them that call on the Lord out of a pure heart."
-II Timothy 2:22

Ingredient #6—Resisting the Devil

"Submit yourselves therefore to God. Resist the devil, and he will flee from you."
-James 4:7

Ingredients for Balanced Christian Living
Recipe for:
SATAN'S ATTACKS

Ephesians 6:14-18	Putting on God's Armor
Psalm 34:14	Having the right pursuit
1 Corinthians 10:13	Escaping Temptation
1 Thessalonians 5:22	Abstaining from evil
2 Timothy 2:22	Running from lust
James 4:7	Resisting the Devil

Ingredients for Balanced Christian Living

IDENTIFY THE FOLLOWING:

1. What ingredients am I lacking in my fight against Satan's attacks?

2. What ingredients will I add to my life today?

3. What ingredient do I struggle with the most?

Marriage Ingredients

BALANCE IN MARRIAGE

Marriage was in the mind of God from the beginning of time. Marriage was one of the first subjects of the Bible. As previously stated, before ministry, God instituted the family. God's view of marriage is between one man and one woman. He said, "these two become one flesh". The core of marriage involves sacrifice, submission, and honor.

Walking in a godly approach to our marriage must be a lifestyle.

Ingredients for Marriage:

Ingredient #1—Operating as one

"Wherefore they are no more twain, but one flesh. What therefore God hath joined together, let no man put asunder."

-Matthew 19:6

Ingredient #2—Loving as Jesus Christ

"Husbands, love your wives, even as Christ also loved the church, and gave himself for it;"

-Ephesians 5:25

Ingredient #3—Submitting to one another

"Wives, submit yourselves unto you own husbands, as unto the Lord."

-Ephesians 5:22

Ingredient #4—Honoring each other

"Likewise, ye husbands, dwell with them according to knowledge, giving honor unto the wife…"

-I Peter 3:7

Ingredient #5—Communicating with each other

"Defraud ye not one the other, except it be with consent for a time, that ye may give yourselves to fasting and prayer; and come together again, that Satan tempt you not for your incontinency."
-I Corinthians 7:5

Ingredients for Balanced Christian Living
Recipe for:

MARRIAGE

Matthew 19:6	Operating as one
Ephesians 5:25	Loving one another
Ephesians 5:22	Submitting to one another
1 Peter 3:7	Honoring each other
1 Corinthians 7:5	Communicating with each other

Ingredients for Balanced Christian Living

IDENTIFY THE FOLLOWING:

1. What ingredients am I lacking in my marriage?

2. What ingredients will I add to my life today?

3. What ingredient do I struggle with the most?

Prayer & Fasting Ingredients

Balance in Prayer and Fasting

The more time you spend with God allows you to get closer to Him. God wants us to be disciplined in our quest to know Him. We become better disciples of Jesus, when we are disciplined. Prayer and fasting is a disciplined lifestyle that allows the believer to rely more on the spirit than the flesh. We come to know God in a deeper way through prayer and fasting.

Walking in prayer and fasting must be a lifestyle.

Ingredients for Prayer and Fasting:

Ingredient #1—Having a prayer closet

"And when thou prayest, thou shalt not be as the hypocrites are: for they love to pray standing in the synagogues, and in the corners of the streets, that they may be seen of men. Verily I say unto you, they have their reward. But thou, when thou prayest, enter into thy closet, and when thou hast shut thy door, pray to the Father which is in secret; and thy Father which seeth in secret shall reward thee openly. But when ye pray, use not vain repetitions, as the heathen do: for they think that they shall be heard for their much speaking."

-Matthew 6:5-7

Ingredient #2—Unceasing Prayers

"Pray without ceasing."

-I Thessalonians 5:17

Ingredient #3—Being an intercessor

"And I sought for a man among them, that should make up the hedge, and stand in the gap before me for the land, that I should not destroy it: but I found none."

-Ezekiel 22:30

Ingredient #4—Fasting unto God

"Moreover when ye fast, be not, as the hypocrites; of a sad countenance: for they disfigure their faces, that they my appear unto men to fast, Verily is say unto you they have their reward. But thou, when thou fastest, anoint thine head, and wash thy face; That thou appear not unto men to fast, but unto thy Father which is in secret: and thy Father, which seeth in secret, shall reward thee openly."

-Matthew 6:16-18

Ingredient #5—Sacrificing Self

"And when he was come into the house, his disciples asked him privately, Why could not we cast him out? And he said unto them, This kind can come forth by nothing, but by prayer and fasting."

-Mark 9:28, 29

Ingredient #6—Availing Prayers

"Confess your faults one to another, and pray one for another, that ye may be healed. The effectual fervent prayer of a righteous man availeth much."

-James 5:16

Ingredients for Balanced Christian Living Recipe for:

PRAYER AND FASTING

Matthew 6:5-7	Having a prayer closet
1 Thessalonians 5:17	Unceasing Prayer
Ezekiel 22:30	Being an intercessor
Matthew 6:16-18	Fasting unto God
Mark 9:28, 29	Sanctifying Self
James 5:16	Availing Prayers

Ingredients for Balanced Christian Living

IDENTIFY THE FOLLOWING:

1. What ingredients am I lacking in my prayer and fasting?

2. What ingredients will I add to my life today?

3. What ingredient do I struggle with the most?

Neighbor Ingredients

BALANCE IN NEIGHBOR

There will always be a time where we will have to deal with people. Christians are not to deal with people the same way the world does. Christians should maintain a standard of godliness with all people. A measure of Christian maturity is how we deal with our neighbor. Our relationship with Jesus should reflect our relationship with our neighbor.

Walking in a godly approach to our neighbor must be a lifestyle.

Ingredients for Dealing with My Neighbor:

Ingredient #1—Loving your neighbor

"Thou shalt not avenge, nor bear any grudge against the children of thy people, but thou shalt love thy neighbor as thyself: I am the Lord."

-Leviticus 19:18

Ingredient #2—Treating your neighbor as you want to be treated

"Therefore all things whatsoever ye would that men should do to you, do ye even so to them: for this is the law and the prophets."

-Matthew 7:12

Ingredient #3—Living with your neighbor

"If it be possible, as much as lieth in you, live peaceably with all men."

-Romans 12:18

Ingredient #4—Avenge not your neighbor

"Dearly beloved, avenge not yourselves, but rather give place unto wrath: for it is written, Vengeance is mine; I will repay, saith the Lord."

-Romans 12:19

Ingredient #5—Loving your enemy

"But I say unto you, Love your enemies, bless them that curse you, do good to them that hate you, and pray for them which despitefully use you, and persecute you;"

-Matthew 5:44

Ingredient #6—Being fair to your neighbor

"Judge not, that ye be not judged. For with what judgment ye judge, ye shall be judged: and with what measure ye mete, it shall be measured to you again."

-Matthew 7:1, 2

Ingredients for Balanced Christian Living
Recipe for:

NEIGHBOR

Leviticus 19:18	Loving your neighbor
Matthew 7:12	Treating your neighbor as you want to be treated
Romans 12:18	Living with your neighbor
Romans 12:19	Avenge not your neighbor
Matthew 5:44	Loving your enemy
Matthew 7:1, 2	Being fair to your neighbor

Ingredients for Balanced Christian Living

IDENTIFY THE FOLLOWING:

1. What ingredients am I lacking with my neighbor?

2. What ingredients will I add to my life today?

3. What ingredient do I struggle with the most?

Forgiveness Ingredients

BALANCE IN FORGIVENESS

God opened the door of forgiveness by sending His only begotten Son to die for the sins our sins. Jesus suffered more for our forgiveness than anyone else. In spite of all His suffering, Jesus never compromised His character. We do not need to ask for forgiveness, but we must walk in that same forgiveness toward others. No matter how much someone hurts us, forgiveness is not an option, but a requirement of God.

Walking in forgiveness must be a lifestyle.

Ingredients for Forgiveness:

Ingredient #1—Forgiving your neighbor

"For if ye forgive men their trespasses, your heavenly Father will also forgive you: But if ye forgive not men their trespasses, neither will your Father forgive your trespasses."
-Matthew 6:14, 15

Ingredient #2—Understanding God's forgiveness

"As far as the east is from the west, so far hath he removed our transgressions from us."
-Psalm 103:12

Ingredient #3—Embracing God's forgiveness

"Bless the Lord, O my soul, and forget not all his benefits. Who forgiveth all thine iniquities; who healeth all thy diseases,"
-Psalm 103:2, 3

Ingredient #4—Forgiving all offences

"So likewise shall my heavenly Father do also unto you, if ye from your hearts forgive not every one his brother their trespasses."

-Matthew 18:35

Ingredients #5—Asking for forgiveness daily

"If we confess our sins, he is faithful and just to forgive us our sins, and to cleanse us from all unrighteous."

-I John 1:9

Ingredient #6—Having compassion

"And he kneeled down, and cried with a loud voice, Lord, lay not this sin to their charge. And when he had said this, he fell asleep."

-Acts 7:60

Ingredients for Balanced Christian Living
Recipe for:

FORGIVENESS

Matthew 6:14, 15	Forgiving your neighbor
Psalm 103:12	Understanding God's forgiveness
Psalm 103:2, 3	Embracing God's forgiveness
Matthew 18:35	Forgiving all offences
1 John 1:9	Asking for daily forgiveness
Acts 7:60	Having compassion

Ingredients for Balanced Christian Living

IDENTIFY THE FOLLOWING:

1. What ingredients am I lacking in my forgiveness?

2. What ingredients will I add to my life today?

3. What ingredient do I struggle with the most?

Grace Ingredients

BALANCE IN GRACE

Grace is God's unmerited favor of God to an individual. God's desire is that we exemplify the humility of Jesus. God gives more grace to those that walk in humility. One may say that our humility is an avenue for God's grace. Believers are not to take for granted or abuse God's loving grace.

Walking in grace must be a lifestyle.

Ingredients for Grace:

Ingredient #1—Displaying humility

"Surely he scorneth the scorners: but he giveth grace unto the lowly."

-Proverbs 3:34

Ingredient 2—Receiving Grace

"But he giveth more grace, wherefore he saith, God resisteth the proud, but giveth grace unto the humble."

-James 4:6

Ingredient #3—Sustaining Grace

"And he said unto me, My grace is sufficient for thee: for my strength is made perfect in weakness. Most gladly therefore will I rather glory in my infirmities, that the power of Christ may rest upon me."

-II Corinthians 12:9

Ingredient #4—Ministering in Grace

"And Stephen, full of faith and power, did great wonders and miracles among the people."

-Acts 6:8

Ingredient #5—Maximizing Grace

"But unto every one of us is given grace according to the measure of the gift of Christ."

-Ephesians 4:7

Ingredient #6—Living under Grace

"For sin shall not have dominion over you: for ye are not under the law, but under grace."

-Romans 6:14

**Ingredients for Balanced Christian Living
Recipe for:**

GRACE

Proverbs 3:34	Displaying humility
James 4:6	Receiving Grace
II Corinthians 12:9	Sustaining Grace
Acts 6:8	Ministering in Grace
Ephesians 4:7	Maximizing Grace
Romans 6:14	Living under Grace

Ingredients for Balanced Christian Living

IDENTIFY THE FOLLOWING:

1. What ingredients am I lacking in my grace?

2. What ingredients will I add to my life today?

3. What ingredient do I struggle with the most?

Love Ingredients

BALANCE IN LOVE

The clearest scripture that identifies the love of an Almighty God is found in John 3:16. God loves us and we are commanded to love others. There are benefits for us when we love. Our love should mirror the love of God. We are to display love to everyone. Scripture does not give us the leeway to choose. The love of God does not separate from us. Therefore our love should not separate from anyone.

Walking in love must be a lifestyle.

Ingredients for Love:

Ingredient #1—Walking in Love

"And walk in love, as Christ also hath loved us, and hath given himself for us an offering and a sacrifice to God for a sweetsmelling savour."

-Ephesians 5:2

Ingredient #2—Loving in deed and in truth

"My little children, let us not love in word, neither in tongue; but in deed and in truth."

-I John 3:18

Ingredient #3—Displaying Love

"If a man say, I love God, and hateth his brother, he is a liar, for he that loveth not his brother who he hath seen, how can he love God whom he hath not seen?"

-I John 4:20

Ingredient #4—Embracing Love for God

"And we know that all things work together for good to them that love God, to them who are the called according to his purpose."

-Romans 8:28

Ingredient #5—Realizing the Power of God's Love

"For I am persuaded, that neither death, nor life, nor angels, nor principalities, nor powers, nor things present, nor things to come. Nor height, nor depth, nor any other creature, shall be able to separate us from the love of God, which is in Christ Jesus our Lord."

-Romans 8:38, 39

Ingredient #6—Having Fervent Love

"And above all things have fervent charity among yourselves: for charity shall cover the multitude of sins."

-I Peter 4:8

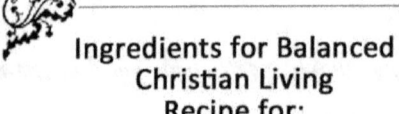  

Ingredients for Balanced Christian Living
Recipe for:

LOVE

Ephesians 5:2	Walking in Love
1 John 3:18	Loving in deed and in truth
1 John 4:20	Displaying Love
Romans 8:28	Embracing Love for God
Romans 8:38, 39	Realizing the Power of God's Love
1 Peter 4:8	Having Fervent Love

Ingredients for Balanced Christian Living

IDENTIFY THE FOLLOWING:

1. What ingredients am I lacking in my love?

2. What ingredients will I add to my life today?

3. What ingredient do I struggle with the most?

Conclusion

In Matthew 5:16 Jesus makes a defining statement for every Christian, He says, *"Let your light so shine before men, that they may see your good works, and glorify your Father which is in heaven."* In order for our lights to shine, we must live a balanced life based on the Word of God. We are to reflect the light of Jesus Christ in our homes and community. We may be the only light that a family member, co-worker, neighbor, or stranger may see in a course of day. Pray daily that God will help add the needed ingredients in your life, so you will shine and grow in Him.

In the book of 1 Kings, the Lord came to Solomon in a dream and asked him, *"What shall I give thee (I Kings 3:5)?"* At this point, Solomon was becoming king over God's people. Solomon responds, *"Give therefore thy servant an understanding heart to judge thy people, that I may discern between good and bad: for who is able to judge this thy so great a people"* (1 Kings 3:9). Solomon asked for godly wisdom to lead the people. Unfortunately, Solomon did not always walk in the wisdom of God. When Solomon realized that his life became unbalanced because of his desire for unhealthy ingredients, he concludes the book of Ecclesiastes saying, *"Let us hear the conclusion of the whole matter: Fear God, and keep his commandments: for this is the whole duty of man (12:13)."* Our lives will stay balanced when we fear God and keep His commandments on a daily basis.

www.ingramcontent.com/pod-product-compliance
Lightning Source LLC
Chambersburg PA
CBHW070624300426
44113CB00010B/1650